Fabulous!

A PORTRAIT OF
ANDY WARHOL

BY BONNIE CHRISTENSEN

Christy Ottaviano Books
Henry Holt and Company • New York

For Andrea—
Andy of the "scavi"

Illustration Note

The paintings in this book are replicas of Andy's paintings, intended to give the reader
a sense of his work and to inspire a museum visit to view the true originals.

Henry Holt and Company, LLC
Publishers since 1866
175 Fifth Avenue
New York, New York 10010
www.HenryHoltKids.com

Library of Congress Cataloging-in-Publication Data
Christensen, Bonnie.
Fabulous : a portrait of Andy Warhol / by Bonnie Christensen. — 1st ed.
p.   cm.
"Christy Ottaviano Books."
Includes bibliographical references.
ISBN 978-0-8050-8753-6
1. Warhol, Andy, 1928–1987—Juvenile literature. 2. Artists—
United States—Biography—Juvenile literature. I. Title.
N6537.W28C49 2011   700.92—dc22   [B]   2010027840

First Edition—2011 / Designed by Elynn Cohen
Collaged photo transfers on canvas, which were then painted in oil,
were used to create the illustrations for this book.

Printed in January 2011 in China by Imago USA, Inc.,
Dongguan City, Guangdong Province, on acid-free paper. ∞

1 3 5 7 9 10 8 6 4 2

"They always say that
time changes things,
but you actually have to
change them yourself."

—Andy Warhol

New York City, 1966

Wow! See that guy with the wild silver wig and the white white skin? An actress on one side, a rock star on the other.

"Oh, Andy, do my portrait!" they beg. Andy sighs and sometimes says, "Yes," or "No," or "I don't know." He never says much, though. He mostly watches. And listens.

Everyone wants to get close to Andy Warhol, Prince of Pop, King of Cool. Photographers line up outside, waiting. The night streets of New York glitter with headlights, streetlights, and flashbulbs.

Pittsburgh, Pennsylvania, 1930s

The streets of New York were a world away from the hillside alleys where Andy grew up. Where his immigrant parents and two brothers worked hard just to get by. The whole family lived in just two rooms, no indoor toilet, and only one bed for three boys. Andy was the baby. Small. Smart. Shy.

On his first day of school a girl hit him. Andy cried and refused to go back. At home he and his mother drew pictures of each other and the family cat.

Two years later, at six, Andy started a new school. His teachers liked him and recognized his talent for drawing. Andy drew constantly. When he was supposed to be covering outfield during a baseball game, his brother found him drawing flowers and butterflies in the front yard.

Illness, Third Grade

Movie magazines, a Charlie McCarthy doll, Dick
Tracy comics, paper dolls, a cap gun—all these
things covered Andy's bed during months of illness.
His illness, Saint Vitus's dance, caused muscle
spasms and permanently blotchy skin. Andy
listened to the radio, his mother read to him, his
brother helped him write fan letters to movie stars.
Shirley Temple sent him a signed photo.

 While he was sick, Andy's bed was in the
middle of the dining room. Glamorous celebrities
and superheroes kept him company. Day after
day Andy drew, watched everything around him,
and drew some more. His mother gave him a
chocolate bar whenever he finished a drawing.
Why should he ever go back to school?

Art

But with a pale, red-blotched face Andy *did* go back to school when he was well enough. Kids called him "Spot." People said he was a sissy because he spent so much time with his mother and refused to catch a football. He drew through it all.

Andy drew during free art classes at the Carnegie Museum. "Everything you observe has art, or the lack of art," his teacher said. Andy drew portraits of cousins, portraits of neighbors. He gazed at icon portraits in church. Rows and rows of portraits: The form intrigued him.

High School Years

Andy was thirteen when his father died. The family mourned. Walking to school through the Czech ghetto, Andy felt left out and alone. Marked by his blotchy skin, his red and bumpy nose, everyone, even his family, called him "Andy the Red Nosed Warhola." Andy kept his head down, filling whole notebooks with drawings.

College

In college, Andy studied art and invented his own drawing style. He also learned that paintings aren't just decoration. Paintings can make people mad, make them ask questions, make them see things differently.

Why Pick on Me?, Andy's painting of a boy picking his nose, did all those things and was rejected from a major art exhibit. Andy put the painting in another show, and people flocked to see it because of the controversy.

New York City, 1949

Just out of art school, Andy Warhol boarded a night train in Pittsburgh.
He carried his portfolio of drawings and two hundred dollars. "You will do
something Great! Crazy! Terrific!" his mother predicted.

   As the train chugged through the night, Pittsburgh became a tiny spot on
the horizon, then quickly disappeared. "Penn Station," the train conductor
called out at dawn. "New York City!" Andy Warhol was off and running.
Within a week he had his first job, illustrating a magazine story titled
"Success Is a Job in New York." After that, the work never stopped.

The "Cockroach Period"

But success didn't equal fame and fortune. Andy shared a series of shabby apartments with a lot of people (as well as cockroaches). He still felt lonely and didn't have a close friend.

Nights he spent drawing. Days he spent looking for work, dressed like a sloppy college kid. "Raggedy Andy," they called him, but art directors thought his drawings were electrifying. Andy worked hard to please, doing drawings over and over to get them exactly right.

A Home

Illustration work, prestigious awards, and money began to roll in. Andy rented his own apartment and adopted a cat. His mother came for a visit and stayed forever.

Andy kept on drawing, even when he wasn't working. He drew pictures of shoes and food, portraits of friends and his cats—soon too many to count, all named Sam. Because he hated working alone, Andy convinced friends to help him paint his drawings. When he complained about going bald, his friends encouraged him to buy a wig. As time passed, the wigs got wilder and wilder.

1960

Friends, success, money, attention—Andy had them all. It wasn't enough. "I want to be as famous as the Queen of England." He said, "I want to be Matisse."

But Andy was a commercial artist; Matisse, a celebrated fine artist. Commercial art was everywhere—newspapers, magazines, street corners—while fine art hung in twinkling white galleries. Rich and elegant beauties visited galleries, bought fine art paintings, and adored the painters.

Andy looked around. Some fine art galleries were suddenly showing everyday objects, just like commercial art. He'd been training for ten years. Why couldn't he do that?

So he set up a studio and started big paintings—Dick Tracy pieces, ads for wigs, TVs, cans of food, Coke bottles. Some galleries seemed interested. But nothing came of it. Andy worried. "What should I paint?" he asked a friend.

"Paint something so familiar that nobody even notices it," she answered. "Something like a Campbell's Soup can."

Campbell's Soup Cans

Good advice. Andy made thirty-two paintings, one for each kind of Campbell's Soup. A fine art gallery in Los Angeles showed them all lined up side by side. They caused a sensation. Andy was on his way as a fine artist.

Next, Andy painted portraits of movie stars. Then photos from newspapers. He painted portraits of people, objects, and events that defined the times.

The Factory

If one is good, fifty is better. Andy learned to reproduce his paintings quickly. He could make rows and rows of Coca-Cola bottles or portraits. Andy called his studio the Factory because he and his assistants quickly manufactured paintings using a commercial printing process. Friends and strangers stopped by all the time. Andy was always working—never alone.

Then he bought a movie camera. Andy's first films were simply about watching. *Sleep* featured a man sleeping for six hours. *Empire* showed the Empire State Building for eight hours. More shock. More films. More fame.

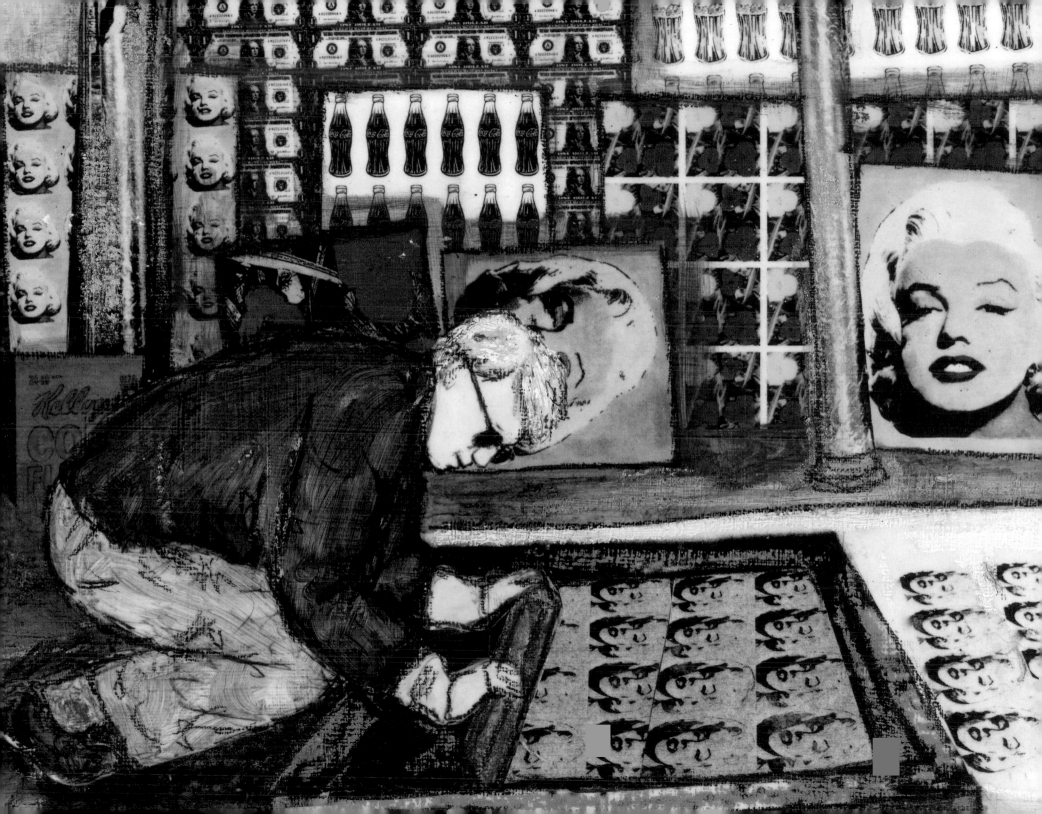

Andy was soon as famous as the movie stars he painted. Famous in New York and Paris, where crowds lined up to see his paintings in glittering fine art galleries.

Famous in Rome, Italy, where he met with the Pope. Famous in Philadelphia, where four thousand people mobbed the opening of his first museum show. "Spot"—the poor, sick, and shy kid from Pittsburgh—had transformed himself into the Prince of Pop Art. Art that anyone could recognize and understand.

Oh, no. Is he going? Heads turn as Andy leaves the restaurant. Most everyone watches him.

"Autograph?" someone asks, holding out a napkin to be signed.

"Sure. Yeah." Andy sighs. He's nice and friendly in a quiet way. He smiles.

Outside, photographers stop him to ask, "Hey, Andy, what's next?"

Andy pauses, looking a bit confused. Everyone waits. After a minute he puts his hand on his mouth and tilts his head to the side.

"I don't know," Andy says softly. "What do you think?"

No one answers.
Flashbulbs flash. Andy
smiles again, a tiny smile,
and slips away along the
glittering night street.
"Fabulous," he whispers
to himself. "Fabulous!"

Author's Note

Andy Warhol—To most people that name conjures images of Campbell's Soup cans and a pale man wearing an outrageous wig. Some recall the phrase, "In the future everyone will be famous for fifteen minutes."

Very few people know that Andy Warhol attended church regularly, helped serve Thanksgiving dinners to the homeless, lived most of his adult life with his mother, and possibly suffered from dyslexia or Asperger's syndrome.

Warhol truly did things his way. When having trouble tying a necktie, he'd simply cut off the end that gave him difficulty and stuff it in a box filled with cut-off tie bits. He also used cardboard boxes to store the ephemera he acquired on a daily basis—newspapers, fan letters, bits and pieces of this and that. He called these boxes "time capsules" and created over 600 of them.

Besides his unique perspective and imagination, Andy also had a sense of humor. Once, trying to find illustration work, he called a magazine and said, "Hello. This is Andy Warhol. I planted some birdseed in the park today. Would you like to order a bird?" Then he asked for a job.

In the final analysis, Warhol appeals on many levels. Warhol the artist broke down barriers. Warhol the poor kid from Pittsburgh was sought out by all sorts of stars. Warhol coyly stonewalling interviewers and toying with the press. He was a man of few words, who was apt to seek ideas for his artwork from all sources. A man who worked constantly but had an air of diffidence that could lead one to believe he never labored a day. Full of contradictions, both stated and implied. Fascinating and fabulous!

Bibliography

Andy Warhol, Drawings and Illustrations of the 1950s. New York: D.A.P./Goliga Books, 2000.
Bourdon, David. *Warhol*. New York: Harry Abrams, 1995.
Greenberg, Jan, and Sandra Jordan. *Andy Warhol, Prince of Pop*. New York: Laurel-Leaf, 2007.
Honnef, Klaus. *Andy Warhol, 1928–1987: Commerce into Art*. Translated by Carole Fahy and I. Burns. Cologne, Germany: Taschen Verlag, 2000.
Rubin, Susan Goldman. *Andy Warhol: Pop Art Painter*. New York: Abrams Books for Young Readers, 2006.
Warhol, Andy. *The Philosophy of Andy Warhol: From A to B and Back Again*. San Diego: Harcourt Brace Jovanovich, 1975.
Warhol, James. *Uncle Andy's*. New York: Putnam, 2003.

Warhol Time Line

1928

Andrew Warhola (he later dropped the final *a*) is born on August 6 to Andrej and Julia Warhola in Pittsburgh, Pennsylvania. He has two older brothers, Paul and John.

1934

Attends grade school, skipping first grade. Has some difficulty with reading, now believed to have been dyslexic.

1936

Becomes ill with Saint Vitus's dance, a nerve disorder that causes muscle spasms and results in pale, blotchy skin.

1937-41

Attends free art classes at the Carnegie Institute.

1942

His father dies after a three-year illness.

1945

Graduates from Schenley High School.

1949

Graduates from college, Carnegie Institute of Technology, and moves to New York City. He immediately gets illustration work, and his career flourishes. His first illustration credit mistakenly drops the *a* from the end of Warhola. Andy continues to work as "Warhol."

1950

His mother moves in with Andy. She does hand-lettering for his illustrations and books.

1960

Buys a townhouse in New York, where he lives and works. Makes his first comic strip paintings.

1962

Paints dollar bills and Campbell's Soup cans. Exhibits at Ferus Gallery in Los Angeles. Exhibits at Sidney Janis Gallery in New York.

1963

Buys a movie camera and begins making films; over the following years he makes seventy-five movies. Rents a studio, the Factory. First solo exhibit in Europe. Makes first cardboard box sculptures.

1965

First solo museum exhibition in Philadelphia.

1968

A deranged woman, Valerie Solanis, walks into the Factory and shoots Andy. He barely survives.

1969

Andy publishes the first edition of his magazine, *Interview*.

1972

Andy focuses again on paintings of a variety of subjects. His mother dies in Pittsburgh.

1975

The Philosophy of Andy Warhol: From A to B and Back Again is published.

1980

Works on *Andy Warhol's TV*, a TV show, and publishes *POPisms: The Warhol Sixties*, written by Andy and Pat Hackett.

1987

Andy Warhol dies on February 22 after routine surgery. The courts estimate his estate to be worth $220 million.